Property of
Walnut Township Memorial Library
Walnut, Ill.

S0-ASE-980

Property of
Walnut Township Memorial Library
Walnut, Illinois

KNOW YOUR GOVERNMENT

The Department of the Interior

353.3
CLK
2 7538

The Department of the Interior

Fred Clement

CHELSEA HOUSE PUBLISHERS

Chelsea House Publishers
Editor-in-Chief: Nancy Toff
Executive Editor: Remmel T. Nunn
Managing Editor: Karyn Gullen Browne
Copy Chief: Juliann Barbato
Picture Editor: Adrian G. Allen
Art Director: Maria Epes
Manufacturing Manager: Gerald Levine

Know Your Government
Senior Editor: Kathy Kuhtz

Staff for THE DEPARTMENT OF THE INTERIOR
Assistant Editor: Gillian Bucky
Copy Editor: Karen Hammonds
Deputy Copy Chief: Ellen Scordato
Editorial Assistant: Theodore Keyes
Picture Researcher: Ed Dixon
Assistant Art Director: Laurie Jewell
Senior Designer: Noreen M. Lamb
Production Coordinator: Joseph Romano

Copyright © 1989 by Chelsea House Publishers, a division of Main Line Book Co. All
rights reserved. Printed and bound in the United States of America.

First Printing

1 3 5 7 9 8 6 4 2

Library of Congress Cataloging in Publication Data

Clement, Fred.
  The Department of the Interior.

  (Know your government)
  Bibliography: p.
  Includes index.
  Summary: Surveys the history of the Department of the Interior with descriptions
of its structure, current function, and influence on society.
  1. United States. Dept. of the Interior—Juvenile literature. [1. United States.
Dept. of the Interior] I. Title. II. Series: Know your government (New York, N.Y.)
JK868.C58 1988   353.3   87-38216
ISBN 0-87754-842-0
      0-7910-0858-4 (pbk.)

CONTENTS

KNOW YOUR GOVERNMENT

CHELSEA HOUSE PUBLISHERS

INTRODUCTION

Government: Crises of Confidence

Arthur M. Schlesinger, jr.

From the start, Americans have regarded their government with a mixture of reliance and mistrust. The men who founded the republic did not doubt the indispensability of government. "If men were angels," observed the 51st Federalist Paper, "no government would be necessary." But men are not angels. Because human beings are subject to wicked as well as to noble impulses, government was deemed essential to assure freedom and order.

At the same time, the American revolutionaries knew that government could also become a source of injury and oppression. The men who gathered in Philadelphia in 1787 to write the Constitution therefore had two purposes in mind. They wanted to establish a strong central authority and to limit that central authority's capacity to abuse its power.

To prevent the abuse of power, the Founding Fathers wrote two basic principles into the new Constitution. The principle of federalism divided power between the state governments and the central authority. The principle of the separation of powers subdivided the central authority itself into three branches—the executive, the legislative, and the judiciary—so that "each may be a check on the other." The *Know Your Government* series focuses on the major executive departments and agencies in these branches of the federal government.

The Constitution did not plan the executive branch in any detail. After vesting the executive power in the president, it assumed the existence of "executive departments" without specifying what these departments should be. Congress began defining their functions in 1789 by creating the Departments of State, Treasury, and War. The secretaries in charge of these departments made up President Washington's first cabinet. Congress also provided for a legal officer, and President Washington soon invited the attorney general, as he was called, to attend cabinet meetings. As need required, Congress created more executive departments.

Setting up the cabinet was only the first step in organizing the American state. With almost no guidance from the Constitution, President Washington, seconded by Alexander Hamilton, his brilliant secretary of the treasury, equipped the infant republic with a working administrative structure. The Federalists believed in both executive energy and executive accountability and set high standards for public appointments. The Jeffersonian opposition had less faith in strong government and preferred local government to the central authority. But when Jefferson himself became president in 1801, although he set out to change the direction of policy, he found no reason to alter the framework the Federalists had erected.

By 1801 there were about 3,000 federal civilian employees in a nation of a little more than 5 million people. Growth in territory and population steadily enlarged national responsibilities. Thirty years later, when Jackson was president, there were more than 11,000 government workers in a nation of 13 million. The federal establishment was increasing at a faster rate than the population.

Jackson's presidency brought significant changes in the federal service. He believed that the executive branch contained too many officials who saw their jobs as "species of property" and as "a means of promoting individual interest." Against the idea of a permanent service based on life tenure, Jackson argued for the periodic redistribution of federal offices, contending that this was the democratic way and that official duties could be made "so plain and simple that men of intelligence may readily qualify themselves for their performance." He called this policy rotation-in-office. His opponents called it the spoils system.

In fact, partisan legend exaggerated the extent of Jackson's removals. More than 80 percent of federal officeholders retained their jobs. Jackson discharged no larger a proportion of government workers than Jefferson had done a generation earlier. But the rise in these years of mass political parties gave federal patronage new importance as a means of building the party and of rewarding activists. Jackson's successors were less restrained in the distribu-

8

tion of spoils. As the federal establishment grew—to nearly 40,000 by 1861—
the politicization of the public service excited increasing concern.

After the Civil War the spoils system became a major political issue.
High-minded men condemned it as the root of all political evil. The spoilsmen,
said the British commentator James Bryce, "have distorted and depraved the
mechanism of politics." Patronage, by giving jobs to unqualified, incompetent,
and dishonest persons, lowered the standards of public service and nourished
corrupt political machines. Office-seekers pursued presidents and cabinet
secretaries without mercy. "Patronage," said Ulysses S. Grant after his
presidency, "is the bane of the presidential office." "Every time I appoint
someone to office," said another political leader, "I make a hundred enemies
and one ingrate." George William Curtis, the president of the National Civil
Service Reform League, summed up the indictment. He said,

> The theory which perverts public trusts into party spoils, making public
> employment dependent upon personal favor and not on proved merit,
> necessarily ruins the self-respect of public employees, destroys the
> function of party in a republic, prostitutes elections into a desperate
> strife for personal profit, and degrades the national character by lower-
> ing the moral tone and standard of the country.

The object of civil service reform was to promote efficiency and honesty in
the public service and to bring about the ethical regeneration of public life. Over
bitter opposition from politicians, the reformers in 1883 passed the Pendleton
Act, establishing a bipartisan Civil Service Commission, competitive examina-
tions, and appointment on merit. The Pendleton Act also gave the president
authority to extend by executive order the number of "classified" jobs—that is,
jobs subject to the merit system. The act applied initially only to about 14,000
of the more than 100,000 federal positions. But by the end of the 19th century
40 percent of federal jobs had moved into the classified category.

Civil service reform was in part a response to the growing complexity of
American life. As society grew more organized and problems more technical,
official duties were no longer so plain and simple that any person of intelligence
could perform them. In public service, as in other areas, the all-round man was
yielding ground to the expert, the amateur to the professional. The excesses
of the spoils system thus provoked the counter-ideal of scientific public administration, separate from politics and, as far as possible, insulated against it.

The cult of the expert, however, had its own excesses. The idea that
administration could be divorced from policy was an illusion. And in the realm
of policy, the expert, however much segregated from partisan politics, can

9

never attain perfect objectivity. He remains the prisoner of his own set of values. It is these values rather than technical expertise that determine fundamental judgments of public policy. To turn over such judgments to experts, moreover, would be to abandon democracy itself; for in a democracy final decisions must be made by the people and their elected representatives. "The business of the expert," the British political scientist Harold Laski rightly said, "is to be on tap and not on top."

Politics, however, were deeply ingrained in American folkways. This meant intermittent tension between the presidential government, elected every four years by the people, and the permanent government, which saw presidents come and go while it went on forever. Sometimes the permanent government knew better than its political masters; sometimes it opposed or sabotaged valuable new initiatives. In the end a strong president with effective cabinet secretaries could make the permanent government responsive to presidential purpose, but it was often an exasperating struggle.

The struggle within the executive branch was less important, however, than the growing impatience with bureaucracy in society as a whole. The 20th century saw a considerable expansion of the federal establishment. The Great Depression and the New Deal led the national government to take on a variety of new responsibilities. The New Deal extended the federal regulatory apparatus. By 1940, in a nation of 130 million people, the number of federal workers for the first time passed the 1 million mark. The Second World War brought federal civilian employment to 3.8 million in 1945. With peace, the federal establishment declined to around 2 million by 1950. Then growth resumed, reaching 2.8 million by the 1980s.

The New Deal years saw rising criticism of "big government" and "bureau-cracy." Businessmen resented federal regulation. Conservatives worried about the impact of paternalistic government on individual self-reliance, on community responsibility, and on economic and personal freedom. The nation in effect renewed the old debate between Hamilton and Jefferson in the early republic, although with an ironic exchange of positions. For the Hamiltonian constituency, the "rich and well-born," once the advocate of affirmative government, now condemned government intervention, while the Jeffersonian constituency, the plain people, once the advocate of a weak central government and of states' rights, now favored government intervention.

In the 1980s, with the presidency of Ronald Reagan, the debate has burst out with unusual intensity. According to conservatives, government intervention abridges liberty, stifles enterprise, and is inefficient, wasteful, and arbitrary. It disturbs the harmony of the self-adjusting market and creates worse troubles than it solves. Get government off our backs, according to the popular cliché, and our problems will solve themselves. When government is necessary, let it be at the local level, close to the people. Above all, stop the inexorable growth of the federal government.

In fact, for all the talk about the "swollen" and "bloated" bureaucracy, the federal establishment has not been growing as inexorably as many Americans seem to believe. In 1949, it consisted of 2.1 million people. Thirty years later, while the country had grown by 70 million, the federal force had grown only by 750,000. Federal workers were a smaller percentage of the population in 1985 than they were in 1955—or in 1940. The federal establishment, in short, has not kept pace with population growth. Moreover, national defense and the postal service account for 60 percent of federal employment.

Why then the widespread idea about the remorseless growth of government? It is partly because in the 1960s the national government assumed new and intrusive functions: affirmative action in civil rights, environmental protection, safety and health in the workplace, community organization, legal aid to the poor. Although this enlargement of the federal regulatory role was accompanied by marked growth in the size of government on all levels, the expansion has taken place primarily in state and local government. Whereas the federal force increased by only 27 percent in the 30 years after 1950, the state and local government force increased by an astonishing 212 percent.

Despite the statistics, the conviction flourishes in some minds that the national government is a steadily growing behemoth swallowing up the liberties of the people. The foes of Washington prefer local government, feeling it is closer to the people and therefore allegedly more responsive to popular needs. Obviously there is a great deal to be said for settling local questions locally. But local government is characteristically the government of the locally powerful. Historically, the way the locally powerless have won their human and constitutional rights has often been through appeal to the national government. The national government has vindicated racial justice against local bigotry, defended the Bill of Rights against local vigilantism, and protected natural resources against local greed. It has civilized industry and secured the rights of labor organizations. Had the states' rights creed prevailed, there would perhaps still be slavery in the United States.

The national authority, far from diminishing the individual, has given most Americans more personal dignity and liberty than ever before. The individual freedoms destroyed by the increase in national authority have been in the main

11

the freedom to deny black Americans their rights as citizens; the freedom to put small children to work in mills and immigrants in sweatshops; the freedom to pay starvation wages, require barbarous working hours, and permit squalid working conditions; the freedom to deceive in the sale of goods and securities; the freedom to pollute the environment—all freedoms that, one supposes, a civilized nation can readily do without.

"Statements are made," said President John F. Kennedy in 1963, "labelling the Federal Government an outsider, an intruder, an adversary. . . . The United States Government is not a stranger or not an enemy. It is the people of fifty states joining in a national effort. . . . Only a great national effort by a great people working together can explore the mysteries of space, harvest the products at the bottom of the ocean, and mobilize the human, natural, and material resources of our lands."

So an old debate continues. However, Americans are of two minds. When pollsters ask large, spacious questions—Do you think government has become too involved in your lives? Do you think government should stop regulating business?—a sizable majority opposes big government. But when asked specific questions about the practical work of government—Do you favor social security? unemployment compensation? Medicare? health and safety standards in factories? environmental protection? government guarantee of jobs for everyone seeking employment? price and wage controls when inflation threatens?—a sizable majority approves of intervention.

In general, Americans do not want less government. What they want is more efficient government. They want government to do a better job. For a time in the 1970s, with Vietnam and Watergate, Americans lost confidence in the national government. In 1964, more than three-quarters of those polled had thought the national government could be trusted to do right most of the time. By 1980 only one-quarter was prepared to offer such trust. But by 1984 trust in the federal government to manage national affairs had climbed back to 45 percent.

Bureaucracy is a term of abuse. But it is impossible to run any large organization, whether public or private, without a bureaucracy's division of labor and hierarchy of authority. And we live in a world of large organizations. Without bureaucracy modern society would collapse. The problem is not to abolish bureaucracy, but to make it flexible, efficient, and capable of innovation.

Two hundred years after the drafting of the Constitution, Americans still regard government with a mixture of reliance and mistrust—a good combination. Mistrust is the best way to keep government reliable. Informed criticism is the means of correcting governmental inefficiency, incompetence, and arbitrariness; that is, of best enabling government to play its essential role. For without government, we cannot attain the goals of the Founding Fathers. Without an understanding of government, we cannot have the informed criticism that makes government do the job right. It is the duty of every American citizen to know our government—which is what this series is all about.

Colorado's Rocky Mountain National Park boasts 11,000-foot-high peaks and many scenic lakes and waterfalls. The Department of the Interior guards the park and many of America's other natural treasures from the dangers of commercial development.

ONE

Preserving America

Managing the nation's abundant natural resources and preserving its rich cultural heritage are the responsibilities of the Department of the Interior (DOI). From developing the frontier into farmland in the 19th century to leasing offshore oil today, the department has adjusted its role to fit a growing nation's needs. Located in Washington, D.C., the DOI's chief duties include preserving wildlife, managing the largest system of national parks in the world, fostering wise use of land, water, and mineral resources, and encouraging the advancement of Native Americans. Each of these concerns occupies an independent division within the DOI, with its own specific responsibilities. Yet these seemingly disparate divisions are interrelated through the overall purpose of the department.

Established in 1849, the DOI was at first an orphanage for various government offices that handled matters inside the states' and territories' physical borders, such as patents, pensions, and Indian affairs. These matters and others that fit nowhere else in the existing government structure were assigned to the DOI.

Later, as the United States expanded its borders through settlement, war, and land purchases, the DOI supported settlers and the government in their efforts, making national growth a high priority. When prospectors went west and found gold, silver, and coal, the DOI fostered utilization of those natural resources as well. In fact, in 1928 Secretary of the Interior Roy O. West told Congress that during those years an appropriate name for his agency might have been the "Department of Western Development."

Toward the end of the 19th century, however, the public began to realize that farmlands and natural resources would not last forever. The Interior Department responded by evolving into a conservationist organization, undertaking measures to efficiently manage the nation's resources and to preserve the natural environment for future enjoyment. The DOI sponsored scientific explorations of the wilderness, and when Congress created America's first national park in 1872 the department assumed what would soon become one of its major roles—trusteeship of the national park system. The DOI also supervised reforestation and irrigation projects and recognized the importance of preserving America's historical monuments.

In the middle of the 20th century, the department's attention shifted yet again, this time to focus on the dangers of new man-made materials and the

In the mid-19th century, pioneers traveled the 2,000-mile-long Oregon Trail west from Independence, Missouri, in search of rich farmlands in the Pacific Northwest. As the nation's frontier moved westward, legislators recognized the need for a department to supervise the nation's growth.

A U.S. Fish and Wildlife Service (USFWS) employee weighs a bird using a portable scale. The USFWS, responsible for preserving the nation's fish and wildlife and their habitats, is just one of the many conservation agencies under the jurisdiction of the DOI.

overabundance of pollutants in the environment. Environmental protection—keeping the existing environment safe from poisons and pollution—joined conservation as a major concern of the Interior Department.

As modern civilization encroaches upon the wilderness and the demand for use of America's natural resources becomes ever more urgent, today's Interior Department must maintain a delicate balance between preservation and progress. The DOI's efforts to achieve this difficult goal and at the same time maintain a high quality of life for present and future generations of Americans are in keeping with the department's original mission. The DOI has helped the country develop and expand and has, at the same time, worked to keep intact the value and beauty of the nation's natural resources and environment. Despite its various roles, the department's ultimate responsibility continues to be the preservation of the American heritage.

Westward-bound pioneers park their covered wagons and make camp for the night. Territorial expansion increased the demands on the General Land Office of the Treasury Department, spurring support for a new department to handle land policy.

TWO

The Creation of the DOI

On the last evening of the last session of the 30th U.S. Congress in 1849, the Senate resumed debate on a few remaining pieces of legislation. One was a House-approved proposal to create the sixth department of government with cabinet status, called the Home Department or the Department of the Interior. One of its functions would be to administer the young nation's interior—the vast, growing territory reaching into the mountains and plains of the West.

South Carolina senator John C. Calhoun—a powerful former secretary of state and secretary of war—was vehemently opposed to the proposal. "This thing ought not to be," he told his Senate colleagues. "This is a monstrous bill. It is ominous." Calhoun and others who agreed with him worried that such a department would trespass on states' rights. Although the states together formed a nation, each had special needs, and each lawmaker jealously guarded his own state's identity and right to pursue its best interests. Some legislators were wary of measures that threatened to increase federal authority at the expense of states' rights; Calhoun voiced this concern when he stated that proposals for an interior department were "made with a view to bring the people of the country under the supervision of the federal power."

Other legislators were in favor of creating an interior department. They argued that because the nation was constantly growing and changing, the government should evolve along with it. Nevertheless, opponents remained

19

Senator John C. Calhoun, a champion of states' rights throughout his political career, opposed the creation of the Department of the Interior during the 1849 congressional debate. Calhoun argued that a home department would shift power formerly held by states to the federal government.

doubtful. Ohio senator William Allen noted that the government had managed "most triumphantly" since its birth without an interior department. The present number of departments, Allen argued, was sufficient. "The government," he said, "has got along in peace and war with our present departments. They have got along most triumphantly, and I never heard til today that . . . it was necessary to add another member to the cabinet."

Early Proposals for a Home Department

It was true that for more than 60 years the government had functioned with only 5 executive departments. The departments of State, War, Treasury, and Post Office were created in 1789 and the Department of the Navy in 1798. However, as early as the Constitutional Convention of 1787 legislators had proposed a home department. At the convention New York's Gouverneur Morris, a member of the Continental Congress and later a senator, suggested a cabinet-style organization called the Council of State, headed by a secretary of domestic affairs. But Congress reasoned that the benefits of one more executive department would not compensate for the extra salaries and bureaucracy it would create. And so in the nation's early years, Congress had instead divided up internal affairs among the existing departments.

Before the outbreak of the War of 1812, a House of Representatives committee studying administrative problems in Patent Office operations made a similar suggestion. (A patent is a government guarantee that an inventor will have exclusive rights to make, use, or sell his or her invention for a certain period of time.) Patents were then administered by the Department of State. However, as Thomas Jefferson discovered when he was secretary of state (1790–93), Patent Office matters occupied so much of his time that he was unable to concentrate exclusively on state-related matters. Similar problems appeared in the other departments that handled internal affairs because these affairs had little connection to the departments' primary functions.

In 1816, President James Madison endorsed the creation of a home department as part of the proposed administrative reforms contained in the *Cabinet Report of 1816*. The next year, the proposal went to Congress when New York senator Nathan Sanford presented a bill to the Senate to establish a home department. Sanford's bill failed to gain approval, but many statesmen recommended the creation of a sixth department again during James Monroe's presidency (1817–25). Into the late 1820s and 1830s, Congress continued to hear similar proposals but refused to accept any of them.

Territorial Expansion and the Need for a Home Department

Mississippi senator Jefferson Davis suggested in 1849 that it was time to agree on a proposal for a home department. He struggled to convince his Senate colleagues that an expansion of the federal government's jurisdiction was necessary to meet the demands of the future. Ironically, 12 years later Davis would be elected president of the Confederate States of America when the South seceded from the Union to protect the Southern rights and culture that federal authority threatened to abolish.

Senator Henry S. Foote, also from Mississippi, agreed with Davis. He believed that the government had indeed managed well without an interior

Mississippi senator Jefferson Davis led the debate for the creation of a home department. Davis, who would later serve as president of the Confederate States of America, argued that the federal government would not be able to meet increasing internal demands without the addition of such a department.

department. Foote argued, however, that what had worked in the past was no longer working in the present. To deny the creation of a new department simply because it was not necessary in the past "would cut off all future improvement in government," he said, "and compel us to remain stationary whilst the whole world is in progress before us." Foote further explained that

> a full-grown man cannot be expected to wear the clothes which were
> purchased for him in boyhood; and a great nation like ours must expect
> to incur a little more expense in executing the high task of
> self-government than it was necessary to encounter in the earlier stages
> of its existence.

Foote urged the senators to remember that the growing nation now had a population of 20 million people and that commercial, manufacturing, and agricultural resources had expanded proportionately. The governmental machinery must also modify and expand, he concluded.

Mississippi senator Henry Stuart Foote joined with Jefferson Davis to assure Senate passage of the bill creating the Department of the Interior. Foote successfully argued that the federal government needed to expand to cope with the demands of the country's growing territory and population.

For example, the General Land Office, which sold land to the public, was still a bureau of the Treasury Department, where Congress had placed it in 1812. Congress had reasoned that because the land office brought in revenue, the Treasury Department was the appropriate place for it. Foote explained, however, that this relationship was no longer working, because the function of the General Land Office had changed dramatically. The office was now responsible for managing increasing land disputes and legal claims as well as a high volume of property sales.

The United States had expanded rapidly since the turn of the century. The purchase of the Louisiana territory from France in 1803 and the acquisition of Florida from Spain in 1819 significantly increased the country's size. Eager for

The Erie Canal opened in 1825, providing a waterway that carried settlers west from Albany to Buffalo. The canal encouraged western settlement by providing quicker and cheaper passage to the frontier.

John C. Frémont's expeditions in the 1840s to the Oregon country and his detailed topographic reports paved the way for settlement and development of the Pacific Northwest.

financial and territorial growth, the government established liberal land policies. As soon as land became available, settlers bought it. The Land Act of 1800 set a $2-per-acre price on public land, reduced the minimum purchase from 640 to 320 acres, and allowed partial payments over a 4-year period. This new policy made land much more affordable to many farmers and settlers. The Land Act of 1804 reduced the minimum cash payment to $1.64 per acre and authorized 160-acre sales. When the Land Act of 1820 took effect, the price further decreased and sales soared. Pioneers bought small parcels of 80 acres as well as large tracts for as little as $1.25 an acre. Much of the real estate auctioned off in Alabama, Mississippi, and sections of Arkansas and Louisiana spurred settlement in those areas.

When the Erie Canal opened in October 1825, even more settlers pushed westward. Stretching from the city of Albany on the Hudson River to Buffalo on Lake Erie, the canal provided a way west that was both faster and cheaper

U.S. troops engage Mexican soldiers at the Battle of Cerro Gordo in 1847. Under the terms of the Treaty of Guadalupe Hidalgo, which ended the Mexican War, Mexico gave up its claim to Texas and ceded California and New Mexico to the United States.

than any existing overland travel routes. Via this waterway, New Englanders and European immigrants went in search of a new life in the Great Lakes region and beyond. Meanwhile, many families in the middle of the country were gathering their belongings and journeying farther west. New farmland near the Pacific Ocean lured the land hungry, many from Mississippi and Missouri, to Oregon and California. In their zeal to grow cotton in the Mexican territory of Texas, some Americans even placed themselves under Mexican rule. Their subsequent revolt against the Mexican government led to the admission of Texas to the Union in 1845 and eventually to the Mexican War in 1846.

The frontier also offered the promise of freedom to persecuted groups such as the Mormons. Faced with suspicion and violence because of their religious beliefs, which included the practice of *polygyny* (having more than one wife), the Mormons migrated first to Ohio and Missouri and later to Illinois. In 1844, Mormon leader Joseph Smith and his brother were arrested in Carthage, Illinois, after they broke up the printing press of a newspaper in whose pages

Smith had been denounced. A mob broke into the prison where Smith was being held and lynched him. Following this incident, the Mormons sought refuge outside U.S. borders. In 1847, they journeyed to the Great Salt Lake valley in Utah, which was Mexican territory at the time. Mexico ceded Utah to the United States in 1848, at the end of the Mexican War, and Utah became the Mormons' home.

Mass migration populated western territories almost as fast as they were explored. After explorer John C. Frémont's 1843–44 trip from the Missouri River to the Oregon country, settlers from the Mississippi valley—especially Missourians—caught "Oregon fever." Packed into horse-drawn wagons, they traveled along a route that stretched from Independence, Missouri, to the mouth of the Columbia River at Astoria, Oregon. In earlier years, explorers and fur traders had traveled over this Oregon Trail; by 1843, the trail had become the major route to the Pacific Northwest.

At the Anglo-American Convention of 1818, the United States and Great Britain had agreed to share the Oregon territory. In January 1845, however, President James K. Polk, in his first annual message to Congress, claimed all of Oregon as U.S. territory. In 1846, the two nations agreed on a compromise

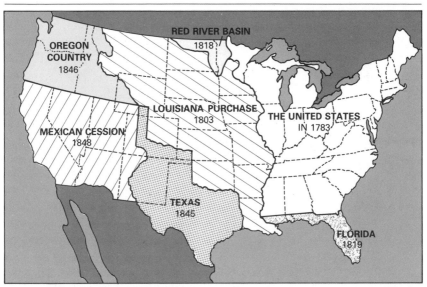

U.S. land acquisition through war, settlement, and purchase, 1783–1848. The nation's incredible rate of growth during the first half of the 19th century led to difficulties in administering U.S. land policy.

to divide the Oregon country. Great Britain gave up claim to the land south of the 49th parallel, and the boundary between Canada and the United States was extended to the Pacific Ocean. Movement on the Oregon Trail increased, and in 1848 Oregon officially became a U.S. territory.

Settlement was just one way in which the United States was expanding at this time. War was another. In 1836 American settlers in the Mexican territory of Texas, uncomfortable with Mexican rule, rebelled and established the Republic of Texas. The national mood of expansionism in the 1840s led Congress to annex Texas in 1845, setting off boundary disputes with Mexico. The Mexican government soon broke diplomatic ties with the United States, and ensuing military skirmishes led to a U.S. declaration of war on May 11, 1846. The Mexican War lasted until 1848, when Mexico, roundly defeated, gave up claims to Texas above the Rio Grande and ceded California and New Mexico to the United States. The new U.S. territory totaled more than 1.19 million square miles and included the present-day states of Arizona, Nevada, California, and Utah and parts of New Mexico, Colorado, and Wyoming.

The rush to settle these new frontiers benefited the nation in many ways. Through settlement, the country grew larger not only in size but also in

U.S. cavalrymen pursue a band of Indians. In the 1800s, the federal government stationed soldiers in the West to protect settlers from Indian attacks.

Treasury Secretary Robert J. Walker suggested that a new department be formed to oversee the nation's internal affairs and to take charge of the land concerns that threatened to overwhelm the Treasury Department.

President James K. Polk signed the bill creating the Department of the Interior (DOI) on March 3, 1849. In addition to taking over the Treasury Department's General Land Office, the DOI inherited the Bureau of Indian Affairs, the Patent Office, and the Pension Office from other government departments.

population. Its people prospered in new areas. Land sales brought money into the U.S. Treasury and stimulated the national economy. However, rapid national growth also brought new problems. Expansion-related debts continued to mount. The cost of the war with Mexico totaled $97.5 million. In addition, the United States had agreed to pay Mexico $15 million in return for the territory it gained. The government also had to finance cavalries stationed in the West—to protect settlers from Indian attacks—and provide funds to western exploration expeditions it had agreed to sponsor.

The nation's rapid expansion was placing an increasingly unmanageable burden on the Treasury Department's General Land Office. The amount of land, the volume of sales, and conflicts over both skyrocketed past 1812 levels, when the office was first created. A growing number of settlers, Indians, and prospectors were quarreling over land rights and property possession. Conflicting claims of ownership and other land-related legal disputes were multiplying faster than the office could manage. By 1848, land concerns and legal problems threatened the ability of the General Land Office—and thus the Treasury Department—to function.

Robert Walker's Solution

Treasury Secretary Robert J. Walker offered a solution to this pressing problem. The rapidity and scope of the country's growth led Walker to the conclusion that a new department was needed to oversee the nation's internal affairs. Walker envisioned charging this department with the Treasury Department's land concerns and other interior matters—including mining rights, national policies governing expansion into western territories, and problems relating to American Indians.

Walker articulated his ideas in his December 1848 *Annual Report to the House of Representatives.* The country's expansion into new territories, he wrote, had overburdened the Treasury Department and threatened it with collapse. No longer strictly Treasury concerns, land-related matters were becoming too much for his department to bear. Between March 1845 and December 1848, Walker told the House, he himself had rendered judgments on more than 5,000 land-title cases. Furthermore, as expansion into the territories continued, the volume of work would increase. In addition, he noted that his role as a judge in land controversies signaled a significant shift in the Treasury secretary's duties—from financial to judicial. His proposed solution to these problems was to form a new cabinet-level department to take charge of these internal affairs and their growing national impact before the Treasury Department collapsed.

The House Ways and Means Committee prepared legislation that would create a department of the interior and presented it to the full House of Representatives for a vote. The House Agriculture Committee also urged the House to pass the bill. Although the bill had its opponents, it passed the House on February 15 and was presented for Senate vote on March 3—the last day of the 30th U.S. Congress.

Even on this last day, however, opponents kept trying to table the bill, to put it aside for discussion until some time in the future. This, in effect, would have killed its chances of passage in the 30th Congress. Noting that delays were dangerous, Jefferson Davis urged his fellow senators not to propose amendments that would waste valuable time. Nevertheless, opponents offered new proposals until a vote was finally called. Despite opposition, the bill was passed

Gold discovered near Sutter's Mill in California's Sacramento Valley in 1848 triggered the California gold rush.

and rushed to President Polk, who was waiting in the vice-president's office in the Capitol. Polk was following a tradition begun by other presidents—being available on the final evening of a congressional session in order to sign last-minute legislation.

"Had I been a member of Congress I would have voted against it," Polk wrote later in his diary. "Many bills pass Congress every year against which the President would vote were he a member of that body, and which he yet approves and signs." Polk feared that the department's "practical operation will be to draw power from the states, where the Constitution has reserved it," disproportionately increasing the power of the federal government.

In addition to the General Land Office, the Department of the Interior inherited the Bureau of Indian Affairs and the Pension Office from the War Department, and the Patent Office from the Department of State. It also became the administrator of the census and of public buildings and charitable and penal institutions in the District of Columbia. As Robert Walker had suggested, the new Interior Department absorbed many of the government's orphaned domestic agencies.

Meanwhile, in 1848, gold had been discovered in California's Sacramento Valley. Although few people realized it yet, the country's biggest gold rush had started. As fortune seekers swarmed to California, the Department of the Interior's General Land Office was about to assume primary importance and meet its first challenge.

HARPER'S WEEKLY.

JOURNAL OF CIVILIZATION

Vol. XVIII.—No. 915.]   NEW YORK, SATURDAY, JULY 11, 1874.   [WITH A SUPPLEMENT PRICE TEN CENTS.

Entered according to Act of Congress, in the Year 1874, by Harper & Brothers, in the Office of the Librarian of Congress, at Washington.

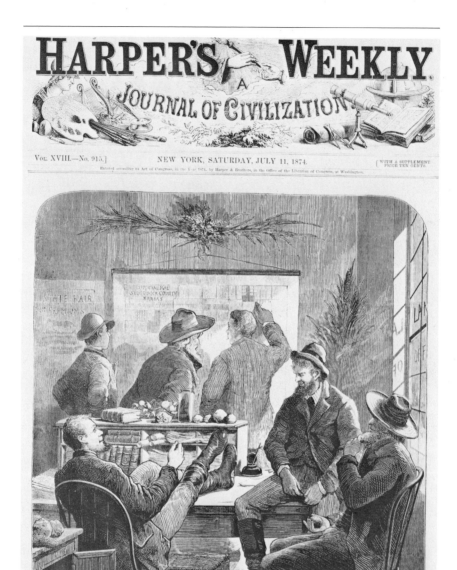

Supervisors in the Kansas land office plan homestead allotments. Between 1862 and 1904 the DOI granted more than 147 million acres of land and sold another 610 million to qualified settlers, under the Homestead Act of 1862.

THREE

The Department of Western Development

A s the newly created Department of the Interior began operations in March 1849, South Carolina senator John C. Calhoun's fear seemed to be coming true. "Everything upon the face of God's earth," he had grumbled during Senate debate, "will go into the Home Department—Indian Affairs, Patent Office, Land Office, Public Buildings, all, all thrown together without the slightest connection." Although it was true that the department was responsible for these various concerns, it would soon emerge foremost as manager of public natural resources and land.

The 1848 gold rush in California focused attention on this vital role. On January 24, James W. Marshall struck gold near present-day Sacramento while building a sawmill for Johann Augustus Sutter, a Swiss immigrant. As word of the discovery spread, gold fever swept across the country. Throughout 1849, adventurers from as far away as China and Australia streamed into the United States. With fortune seekers from this country—farmers, factory workers, lawyers, soldiers, ministers, and outlaws—these men went to find gold. By the end of 1849, an estimated 50,000 to 100,000 people had flocked to California. Within 2 years, they were mining about $51 million worth of gold annually.

A miner travels to the California gold fields. The discovery of gold and other valuable minerals in the West in the mid-1800s sparked a surge of westward expansion that was further encouraged by the Homestead Act of 1862.

In the 1860s and 1870s, gold was found in Colorado, South Dakota, and Nevada—where two small settlements, Humboldt and Esmeralda, became boomtowns. Miners and prospectors struck silver, copper, and coal on public land in other territories, creating a surge in land sales for the Interior Department. Merchants, builders, blacksmiths, and salesmen moved to the new towns and increased the rate of development of the West and its resources.

Since colonial times, native and immigrant farmers and city laborers had looked to the West not only as a land of economic opportunity but as one of greater social and political democracy as well; on the frontier, there were fewer class distinctions and less opposition to extending political privileges to the common man. In his 1860 presidential campaign, Abraham Lincoln recognized this attraction to the West. He called for a homesteading law that would provide settlers with land on government-owned property and thus relieve cities of their increasing burden of disadvantaged immigrants and working-class people. Opening the West was a way, said Lincoln, to provide "places for poor people to go and better their condition."

Federal Land Policy

In 1862, as a result of popular pressure to open up western lands, Congress passed the Homestead Act, which took effect on January 1, 1863, and gave the Interior Department its first major administrative authority. Under this act, any man over 21 years old who was or intended to become a citizen could gain title to 160 acres of surveyed "public domain," or government-owned land. All he had to do was pay a nominal registration fee and live and work on the land for five consecutive years. As an alternative, the act also offered land at a cost of $1.25 per acre with a 6-month residence requirement. Settlers grabbed at these offers. Between 1862 and 1904, homesteaders bought more than 610 million acres and acquired free another 147 million acres. Many of the takers were European immigrants who moved onto the prairies and started wheat farms. They established, almost entirely by themselves, the sugar beet industry.

Through these liberal federal land policies, the Department of the Interior started shaping the West's settlement and the nation's growth. Beginning in the 1860s, population growth in the West was also spurred by the new railroads cutting through the territories. In 1862, Congress passed the Pacific Railway Act, which authorized the construction of a central transcontinental railroad. It was completed in 1869. By the 1890s, four transcontinental railroads were in operation, providing settlers with relatively easy and inexpensive access to new western land.

Surveying the Wilderness

With locomotives chugging across the prairies, Americans rapidly settled the wild West, and the frontier—the region dividing wilderness from settlement—began to disappear. As the availability of new land diminished, settlers' attitudes toward their own land also began to shift. Some worried that uncontrolled exploitation of the West posed a threat to the nation's natural resources and beauty. Certain farmers, for example, realized that reckless agricultural practices were destroying the fertility of the soil. Their concern

A train steams through a western valley. By the 1890s, four railroad companies were providing settlers with easy access to the western territories.

marked the start of a new awareness of conservation, or preservation of the land's appearance and resources.

This outlook corresponded to a new, scientific approach to public land management. Beginning in the late 1860s, independent geologists working with congressional funds launched scientific explorations—called surveys—into the West's mountains, valleys, and plains. These surveys were valuable in mapping, cataloging, and understanding the western wilderness—its geography, geology, climate, and wildlife. Surveys determined, for example, where rivers flowed and whether land was mountainous or suitable for farming. These conclusions, in turn, allowed preparation of effective strategies for developing the West.

The first of four main surveys was headed by Clarence King, a mining engineer and geologist. King explored a 100-mile-wide strip of territory along the axis of the Union Pacific–Central Pacific Railroad, between the Sierra

Geologist-explorer Clarence King led the first large-scale western survey, exploring land between the Sierra Nevada and the Rocky Mountains. King's published records provided valuable information to prospective settlers regarding western climate, soil, and wildlife.

In 1869, explorer John Wesley Powell led a highly publicized expedition down the Colorado River and through the Grand Canyon. Powell's success led to congressional funding for further surveys of the region.

Nevada and the Front Range of the Rocky Mountains, from 1867 to 1873. His report on the expedition, *U.S. Geological Exploration of the Fortieth Parallel*, stimulated public curiosity.

In 1869, John Wesley Powell, a college geology professor and former major in the Union army, led an expedition that captured the public's attention and turned him into a national hero. With partial government funding in the form of rations from western U.S. Army outposts, Powell became the first white man to extensively explore the Green and Colorado rivers. His trip lasted 3 months and covered the 900-mile course of the Grand Canyon and was the last major exploration of its kind to be conducted within the continental United States. Powell's book, *Exploration of the Colorado River of the West and Its Tributaries*, thrilled the public and won him congressional funding for further exploration. In 1874, under the direction of the secretary of the interior and with a $10,000 grant from Congress, Powell began surveying the entire Rocky Mountain region.

Despite the success of the early surveys and the public's burgeoning interest in America's natural treasures, a government agency to oversee such work came into existence only after quarreling broke out between two rival surveys. At about the same time as the King and Powell explorations were taking place, government geologist Ferdinand Hayden was leading a survey of the Rocky

Mountains from the Montana region to Santa Fe. In the process, he collided with a U.S. Army survey commanded by George M. Wheeler. A confrontation developed between the War Department and the civilian scientific community that, in turn, prompted a congressional study of overlapping expenditures. The study recommended the creation of one official geological-survey agency under the auspices of the Department of the Interior.

In 1879 Congress consolidated the surveys into a single, unified western agency, the U.S. Geological Survey. Clarence King became the agency's first director, and from 1880 to 1894 John Wesley Powell headed the organization. Under the Department of the Interior, the agency continued to use science to inform the development of western lands.

The First National Park

During the early 1870s, explorers also launched forays into the Yellowstone area, located in present-day northwestern Wyoming and adjacent parts of Montana and Idaho. Years earlier, trappers, fur traders, and gold prospectors

In 1872, the Yellowstone region of Wyoming—a remarkable area filled with geysers, waterfalls, and wildlife—became America's first national park under the direction of the Department of the Interior.

had told tales of bizarre geysers, hot springs, steamy mud pools, and spectacular cliffs and waterfalls in the region. Later expeditions proved that these tales were true. Working together, explorers, artists, and photographers lobbied Congress to pass a law to maintain the region's dramatic landscapes for the enjoyment of the public, rather than allow it to be staked out privately. In 1872, Congress passed a bill creating Yellowstone National Park. Calling for "the preservation, from injury or spoilation, of all timber, mineral deposits, natural curiosities or wonders within said park and their retention in their natural condition," the act outlined Congress's power to set aside public land as a park or recreation area for public benefit and enjoyment. It placed the first national park under the direction of the Department of the Interior. With this act, the DOI became custodian of the nation's scenic natural resources.

Forests, Deserts, and Historic Landmarks

The Interior Department was also supervising new programs that Congress was initiating through the homesteading laws. In 1873, to foster the growth of trees and forests, Congress adopted the Timber Culture Act, which gave settlers 160 acres if they planted and cultivated 40 acres of trees. Most of this forest-raising activity—covering about 10.8 million acres—occurred in the prairie regions of Kansas and Nebraska.

In the deserts of the West, the challenge for Congress was to adapt the arid and semiarid areas for the use of those trying to homestead there. In western lands, the availability of water—rather than land—was the key to successful settlement. In 1877, Congress promoted irrigation projects through passage of the Desert Land Act, which allowed settlers to buy land at a discount if they could prove they had reclaimed the land through irrigation. The results of this policy, however, were not spectacular: Only about one-third of the attempts to irrigate the desert land succeeded.

A few years later, Secretary of the Interior Carl Schurz attempted to apply conservation methods to save forests. Schurz wanted to stimulate forest replanting and protect federal forest reserves as natural resources. However, he met with opposition from powerful lumber businesses who feared losing the West's prime government-owned timberland. Although the business interests defeated Schurz's plans, his efforts spurred continued interest in forest conservation at the department and enhanced its conservationist role.

Elsewhere, conservation attracted other advocates. In Arizona, for example, scavengers and collectors of ancient artifacts had been destroying a prehistoric

Secretary of the Interior Carl Schurz's attempt to protect the federal forest reserves as a natural resource was thwarted by business interests; however, his efforts in the 1870s provided a preview of the conservationist role the DOI would play in the future.

Indian site, the Casa Grande ruins. In 1889 a group of archaeologists and scientists convinced Congress to authorize repair of the site. Three years later, on the recommendation of Secretary of the Interior John W. Noble, the ruins gained protection as a significant archaeological site. This achievement marked greater DOI responsibility for sites and landmarks of historical value.

Indian Affairs

Although the federal government recognized the historical value of the Casa Grande Indian ruins, taking responsibility for the plight of contemporary American Indians was another matter. In the opinion of the public and the government, Indians were merely adversaries in a battle to open and settle the

West. Since the early 1800s, the U.S. government had practiced a policy of removal and resettlement of Indians. In 1830, with passage of the Indian Removal Act, Congress had called for all eastern Indians to cede their lands and move to unsettled territory west of the Mississippi. Some tribes voluntarily complied with this order; others, however, had to be forcibly evacuated, and a few rose in revolt.

Throughout this era, the Bureau of Indian Affairs (BIA), created in 1824 and placed under the aegis of the War Department, supported and helped carry out the government's resettlement policy. In the mid- to late 1800s, as white settlers moved westward and began to encroach upon the lands set aside for Indian use, the government moved Indians onto *reservations* (areas formally reserved by the federal government specifically for Indian use). The BIA—after 1849 part of the new Department of the Interior—supervised these settlements, which were usually located on land considered undesirable by white settlers. Each reservation was put in the charge of an agent, who

An encampment of Piegan Indians—a Blackfoot tribe—on a reservation in the northern plains region of Montana in the early 19th century. The Bureau of Indian Affairs, part of the DOI after 1849, supervised the settlement of these reservations, which were usually located on land undesirable to white settlers.

An etching of General George A. Custer's last stand at the Battle of the Little Bighorn in 1876. Custer and his entire command were killed by angry Sioux and Cheyenne Indians, led in revolt by Chiefs Sitting Bull and Crazy Horse.

supervised Indian activities and, with his staff, provided economic and social services to the reservation community.

While the BIA oversaw efforts to "civilize" reservation Indians, the U.S. Army battled the tribes that remained free. The Indians' last great victory against U.S. troops occurred in 1876, after General George A. Custer led a U.S. military expedition into the Black Hills of South Dakota—an area granted by treaty to the Sioux Indians—and reported finding gold there. The region was soon swarming with fortune seekers. At the same time, the Northern Pacific Railroad extended a route into the region, further crowding the Indians. Hostilities broke out, and Chiefs Sitting Bull and Crazy Horse led an attack on Custer's troops—later called the Battle of the Little Bighorn—in which Custer and his 225 men were killed. Four months later, U.S. troops defeated the Sioux and moved them onto reservations.

Setbacks continued to plague the Indians. In 1887, Congress passed the Dawes Severalty Act, which ordered the dissolution of many tribes and the division of their reservations among individual members. (*Severalty* refers to

45

property owned by individual right, rather than by shared rights.) According to custom, Indians had always shared their tribal lands. The new law, administered by the BIA, allotted 160 acres to each head of a family and 80 acres to each single adult Indian, destroying the Indians' traditional way of life in an effort to integrate them into white society. As a further indignity, surplus lands left over after allotment were sold to non-Indian settlers.

Reforms in the government's treatment of Indians were eventually made. The 1924 Indian Citizenship Act granted Indians U.S. citizenship and voting rights. In 1926, the secretary of the interior ordered a study of BIA operations. The resulting 1928 *Meriam Report* recommended substantial changes in BIA policy, including the termination of individual land allotment. The report's recommendations were incorporated into the 1934 Indian Reorganization Act (also known as the Wheeler-Howard Act), which ended the practice of land allotment and reinstituted tribal ownership of surplus lands that had been open to sale. The new legislation also provided for the creation of constitutional tribal governments as a basis for restoring tribal unity and self-government. Most important, the act allowed tribes to become economically self-sufficient. The secretary of the interior became trustee of Indian lands, with responsibility for establishing modern conservation practices and development of resources in Indian-owned areas.

"It is merely a beginning," said Commissioner of Indian Affairs John Collier, "in the process of liberating and rejuvenating a subjugated and exploited race living in the midst of an aggressive civilization far ahead, materially speaking, of its own."

Teddy Roosevelt and the Beginnings of Conservation

Meanwhile, the emerging conservation movement of the late 1800s gained greater attention when Theodore Roosevelt became president of the United States in 1901. Roosevelt, a staunch conservationist, made natural resource protection a national concern. In 1902, the Newlands Reclamation Act set aside almost all proceeds from public land sales in 16 western and southwestern states to finance construction and maintenance of irrigation projects in dry states. The act created the Reclamation Service within the Geological Survey to administer the program and authorized the secretary of the interior to allot funds to irrigation projects as he saw fit. In 1903, by executive order, Roosevelt created the first national wildlife refuge, Pelican Island, near Sebastian, Florida.

President Theodore Roosevelt helped to pass a number of measures encouraging the protection and conservation of natural resources. Among his achievements was the creation, in 1903, of the first national wildlife refuge, at Pelican Island in Florida.

More conservation measures followed. Widespread looting of archaeological sites in the Southwest—such as the destruction that took place at Arizona's Casa Grande ruins—spurred Roosevelt to act to protect these national treasures. In 1906, he convinced Congress to pass the Antiquities Act. It gave the president the power to declare historic landmarks and to set aside public land as national monuments—a category that included such natural phenomena as canyons, cliffs, and sand dunes and historic locations such as battlefields and the birthplaces of famous Americans. During the remaining three years of his presidency, Roosevelt designated 1.4 million acres as national monument areas.

Outdoorsman Stephen Mather takes in the view at California's Yosemite National Park in 1918. As special parks assistant to DOI secretary Franklin Lane, Mather successfully lobbied for the creation of the National Park Service and was named the service's first director in 1916.

Creation of the National Park Service

Administering the growing number of national reservations, monuments, and areas of historic and scientific value was becoming difficult at this time. The secretary of the interior, responsible for overseeing each individual park director in addition to discharging his other duties, lacked the time and the resources to devote sufficient attention to the parks. It was becoming clear that a separate office was needed to handle the growing number of problems at the parks.

In 1915, Interior Secretary Franklin K. Lane received a letter from an old friend, Stephen T. Mather, a wealthy businessman and avid outdoorsman. Mather complained to Lane about the way the parks were being run. He had visited the Yosemite and Sequoia areas of the West and was appalled by what he saw there. Souvenir hunters, wildlife poachers, and grazing animals had caused damage to such protected areas for years. In fact, since 1886—in the absence of a protective organization—the First U.S. Cavalry had had to defend

President Franklin D. Roosevelt waves to family and friends as he leaves Warm Springs, Georgia, after a short visit in 1933. Roosevelt worked to promote soil and water conservation, encouraged legislation to protect western lands from overgrazing, and instituted depression-era employment programs that put unemployed Americans back to work and protected the nation's natural resources.

Yellowstone against similar abuses. Impressed by the letter, Lane offered Mather a post as special parks assistant.

Mather immediately set about publicizing the scenic parks in an effort to stimulate public interest and gain increased funding from Congress. He envisioned bringing the uncoordinated system of parks and monuments together under one bureau. His efforts finally paid off in 1916, when Congress passed a bill creating the National Park Service within the Department of the Interior. Congress called on the new bureau

> to conserve the scenery and the natural and historic objects and the wildlife therein and to provide for the enjoyment of the same in such a manner and by such means as will leave them unimpaired for the enjoyment of future generations.

Stephen Mather became the first director of the Park Service. Many of his policies are still in effect today. In several parks, for example, he replaced army administrators with conservation-minded civilian superintendents. He outlawed cattle and sheep grazing and prevented dam building in scenic park waterways.

Secretary of the Interior Harold Ickes, appointed by Roosevelt in 1933, worked closely with the president during the Great Depression. Ickes hired unemployed men to work in conservation-related relief jobs such as the Civilian Conservation Corps (CCC).

A Civilian Conservation Corps (CCC) crew plants pine trees in the Lolo National Forest of Montana. The CCC employed and trained young men in conservation-related labor such as tree planting, road building, and the improvement and upkeep of the national parks.

Foreseeing the importance of the automobile, he made parks easily accessible to them.

Still more changes and new responsibilities were to come to the Interior Department. Like his cousin Theodore, President Franklin D. Roosevelt was a committed conservationist. During his administration (1933–45), guided by Interior Secretary Harold Ickes, Congress passed legislation to protect western lands from cattle grazing and to promote soil and water conservation efforts. Roosevelt also instituted depression-era employment programs such as the Civilian Conservation Corps, which hired thousands of young men to plant trees, build roads and trails, and construct bridges, campgrounds, buildings, and other park improvements. In 1946, the Interior Department's Grazing Service, formed under Roosevelt, merged with the General Land Office to form the Bureau of Land Management.

Upon taking office in 1933, Interior Secretary Ickes assessed his department: "The present Department of the Interior, which was established under an act to create a home department, is as different from the original Department founded in 1849 as the Nation of the gold rush days differs from the Nation of today." The department had indeed changed dramatically since its early days. No longer custodian of orphaned agencies, the DOI was now keeper of a large and powerful nation's precious natural resources.

51

Protesters demonstrate against industrial air pollution in 1969. As awareness of the dangers of pollutants increased in the mid-20th century, the public rallied behind conservationists to lead their movement in a new direction—from preserving the wilderness to protecting the environment from modern industrial pollution.

FOUR

Achievements and Challenges

After World War II, the increasing urbanization of America and the country's growing population, together with the increased volume of visitors to the national parks, threatened to overwhelm the nation's wilderness areas. And conservationists and the DOI renewed their fight against the notion perpetuated by commercial interests that American land had to be "used" for its minerals and other resources.

When President Dwight D. Eisenhower took office in 1953, he appointed Douglas McKay as his secretary of the interior. McKay proved to be no friend to the conservation movement; the prominent conservationist and author Bernard De Voto charged that under McKay's administration the nation's wildlife areas were opened to exploitation that "reversed the conservation policy by which the United States has been working for more than seventy years to substitute wise use of natural resources in place of reckless destruction for the profit of special corporate interests." Conservationists were alarmed when McKay granted an unprecedented number of leases for the extraction of oil and minerals from wildlife refuges and other lands that were under the jurisdiction of the Fish and Wildlife Service. McKay also advocated allowing increased timber cutting on government lands. Moreover, in 1954 he

During Dwight D. Eisenhower's presidency, such issues as civil rights took priority over wilderness preservation. While Eisenhower was in office, renewed commercial activity severely threatened the nation's wilderness areas.

supported controversial legislation that, in the interest of development, posed a threat to a beloved national monument. If approved, the upper Colorado River project would authorize the DOI's Bureau of Reclamation to construct and maintain a system of major dams for irrigation and power in 11 western states. One of the dams was to be located at Echo Park, on the Green River in portions of Colorado and Utah. However, conservationists charged that the proposed Echo Park dam would flood the canyons of the Dinosaur National Monument, a 200,000-acre preserve containing the fossil remains of prehistoric animals.

Wildlife and conservation groups disagreed vehemently with public power advocates. Conservationists claimed that the bill would violate the National Parks Act of 1916, which called for the preservation of "the scenery and the natural and historic objects" located within national parks, monuments, and other protected areas. After a long and emotional battle in Congress, the plan was amended in accordance with the wishes of the public and conservationists, who demanded that Echo Park be stricken from the legislation. When President Eisenhower signed the bill on April 11, 1955, it contained a clause that stated, "It is the intention of Congress that no dam or reservoir constructed under the authorization of this Act shall be within any national park or monument"—a major victory for the park preservationists.

A Bill to Protect the Wilderness

In the late 1940s and throughout the 1950s, there was rising public concern about the continued exploitation of areas already within the network of federally protected lands. National parks, forests, and wildlife preserves were open, at the discretion of federal land administrators, to use by commercial

Dinosaur National Monument was established in 1915 to preserve an area of Colorado and Utah that contains beautiful scenery and a wealth of prehistoric animal remains. Plans to build a dam within the monument in the mid-1950s sparked an enormous protest from conservation groups, which succeeded in blocking construction of the dam.

Visitors stroll through Harpers Ferry National Historical Park, a 2,000-acre Civil War–era site located in Virginia, West Virginia, and Maryland. The construction of visitor services within the national parks in the 1950s led legislators to propose a plan to further restrict activity in many of the remaining undeveloped areas of the park system.

ventures such as mining, logging, and ranching businesses. The nation's shrinking wilderness areas were also threatened by the construction of public and visitor services, including roads, hotels, recreation areas, and reservoirs. Finally, in 1956 legislation to preserve the nation's remaining wilderness areas was introduced in Congress. The Wilderness Bill proposed giving Congress and the president the authority to reserve certain large, undeveloped sections within already existing parks, forests, and wildlife refuges as permanent wilderness areas where no roads, buildings, or other facilities could be constructed and where commercial activities would be restricted.

Predictably, the wilderness legislation was opposed by businesses with a stake in keeping these areas open—logging companies, miners, ranchers who grazed their sheep and cattle on protected lands, and investors in these and other land-use industries. The DOI opposed the bill as well, even though conservation foe Douglas McKay left the department in 1956. Chief among the department's objections was the increased input that the legislation would give

Congress in what was currently a DOI responsibility: deciding how to use the lands located within national parks, forests, and wildlife preserves. The DOI also saw the proposal as particularly untenable for the wildlife refuges because those areas required much closer supervision than the parks or forests.

In the 1960s, however, with support from Presidents John F. Kennedy and Lyndon B. Johnson and with certain concessions to business interests, the wilderness legislation was finally passed. The 1964 Wilderness Act empowered Congress and the president to set aside large, undeveloped tracts in national parks, monuments, and wildlife refuges as part of the wilderness preservation system. The act brought more than 9 million acres of national forest into the wilderness preservation system and provided for the future evaluation and possible inclusion of another 50 million acres of government land. Recognizing the beauty and integrity of America's natural resources, the act declared that

> wilderness . . . in contrast with those areas where man and his own
> works dominate the landscape, is hereby recognized as an area where
> the earth and its community of life are untrammeled by man, where man
> himself is a visitor who does not remain.

In addition to the Wilderness Act, the 1964 Congress passed a number of other conservation bills. Secretary of the Interior Stewart L. Udall, who was

Secretary of the Interior Stewart L. Udall (second from left) visits a coal mine in West Virginia in 1961. Udall promoted conservation legislation during his term as secretary; after leaving office, he wrote about the need to preserve America's land and natural resources.

appointed by President Kennedy in 1961 and served until 1969, proved to be a dedicated wilderness preservationist. Among Udall's efforts to gain congressional funding for national parks, monuments, and recreation areas was his proposal for a fee system for use of previously free recreational areas. The 1964 Land and Water Conservation Fund Act authorized the sale of an automobile windshield sticker that would be required for admission to federal recreational lands and allotted the resulting revenue for the support of recreational planning, land acquisition, and development of federal lands. Considered one of the major pieces of conservation legislation of the 1960s, this act and similar achievements led President Johnson to label the 88th Congress the "Conservation Congress."

Water, Air, and Environmental Protection

In the late 1950s and early 1960s, a growing awareness of the buildup of pollution led the American conservation movement in a new direction. While Congress was acting to protect pristine wilderness areas from development and overuse, legislators were also taking steps to protect the natural environment from the effects of industrial progress.

In 1956, Congress recognized the need for water-quality protection when it passed the Federal Water Pollution Control Act. This act encouraged the development of pollution-control programs, allotted $500 million to help communities build sewage-treatment plants over a 10-year period, and provided for enforcement procedures against noncomplying polluters. Amended in 1961, 1965, and 1969, the law enabled the DOI and other government agencies to prosecute water polluters and set standards for state water-treatment programs. In 1963, Congress passed the Federal Clean Air Act, which provided similar guidelines and funding for controlling air pollution. Amendments further strengthened this act in 1967 and 1970.

In 1962, the country was shocked into an awareness of the extent to which man-made materials were overwhelming the environment. That year, former Fish and Wildlife Service marine-biologist Rachel Carson published *Silent Spring*, a book that focused attention on man-made chemicals, such as pesticides, that were contaminating the environment. *Silent Spring* described the extent to which such pollutants were upsetting ecological systems. Most alarmingly, it called attention to the fact that these dangerous chemicals were not only a risk to soil, air, water, and animal life but also posed a serious danger to humans.

Dead fish, poisoned by industrial pollutants, wash up on a riverbank.
As the dire effects of industrial development on the nation's lands
and wildlife became more pronounced in the 1950s, Congress enacted
legislation to protect these valuable resources.

Carson's book became an immediate best-seller, and a new term—
environmental protection—entered the vocabulary of natural-resource-
protection advocates and began to replace the more familiar term *conservation*.
Then, an incident in early 1969 made the importance of environmental
protection even more evident. Three days after Walter J. Hickel took office as
secretary of the interior, crude oil from a blown-out well in the Santa Barbara
Channel, off the coast of California, bubbled up from the sea bottom. The well
had been drilled on a lease issued by the Interior Department. A vast oil slick
floated ashore, coating the sea and beaches with a black, sticky mess. Large
numbers of seabirds became trapped in the oil, and the region became a
disaster area. While the stunned nation watched, Hickel ordered the drilling
operation shut down and all offshore leasing stopped while the Interior
Department formed new, tighter drilling and production rules.

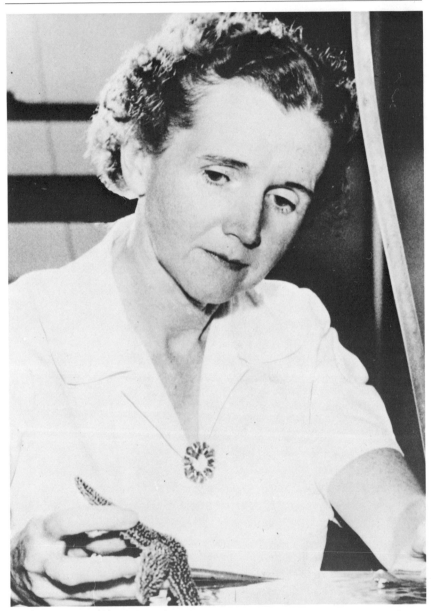

Biologist and writer Rachel Carson ignited the modern environmental protection movement in 1962 when she published Silent Spring, *a warning of the threat posed by man-made chemicals to the health of U.S. lands, wildlife, and citizens.*

State forestry workers rake up oil-soaked straw. Clean straw had been spread on the water to absorb a massive oil spill from a leaking well off the coast of Santa Barbara, California, in 1969. Fatal to marine life and destructive to coastal areas, the disaster was a vivid reminder of the dangers of unbridled industrial development.

By the end of the year, Congress had passed the National Environmental Policy Act (NEPA), a law that made environmental protection a national policy. Hailed by environmentalists as a landmark achievement, NEPA required accountability by federal agencies for actions that would significantly affect the environment. It also gave citizens' groups the power to sue government and industry for any lack of compliance with established standards of environmental protection. Then, in 1970, to coordinate government pollution-control efforts, President Richard Nixon created a new executive department of government, the Environmental Protection Agency (EPA). He assigned it various responsibilities previously handled by government agencies such as the Public Health Service, the Department of Agriculture, and the Department of the Interior. The 1970s proved to be a high point in the passage of conservation legislation; the passage of NEPA and the establishment of the EPA were followed by the passage of a number of landmark pollution-control and conservation acts.

President Richard Nixon created the Environmental Protection Agency in 1970 and charged the new department with coordinating the government's pollution-control programs. Nixon oversaw the enactment of much conservation legislation during his term as president.

Protecting Wildlife

While taking steps to ensure a healthy human environment, Congress also sought to protect wildlife and their habitats. In 1956, Congress created the U.S. Fish and Wildlife Service (USFWS) to study wildlife habitats and the relationships among animals, plants, and insects. The USFWS replaced the old Fish and Wildlife Service, which had been formed in 1940 by the merger within the DOI of the Agriculture Department's Biological Survey and the Commerce Department's Bureau of Fisheries.

The USFWS was charged with monitoring and protecting fish and wildlife and their habitats. Certain human activities, such as urbanization, hunting, and pollution, pose a danger to animal species. The USFWS was created to help these animal populations maintain a biological balance—to protect their population levels from dropping to the point of extinction.

In 1969, Congress passed the Endangered Species Act. This legislation authorized the secretary of the interior to publish a list of endangered species (species that seemed likely to die out); products made from these animals were then banned from import into the United States. In 1972, President Nixon proposed new legislation that made killing of domestic endangered species a federal offense; it was enacted in 1973. Federal agencies including the USFWS have used this law to save many American animal species from extinction.

One example of a success story in saving a dying species is the dramatic comeback of the alligator. About a century ago, the alligator was a common sight in many southern states. In the mid-20th century, however, hunters began relentlessly killing the animal for its skin, which could be made into tough leather. Hunters often stalked alligators at night using the bull's-eye technique: They would shine a light into the animal's eyes, which reflected orange-red and made the animal easy to see and then to kill with a rifle shot or an ax blow to

The U.S. Fish and Wildlife Service protects animals, such as these grizzly bears, in their natural habitat.

An alligator in Florida's Everglades National Park. At one time in danger of extinction, the alligator is now restored to stable population levels in many southern states.

the head. Alligator populations began to shrink rapidly, and by the 1960s the U.S. alligator population had fallen to an alarmingly low level.

Placed on a list of species in danger of extinction in 1967, the alligator was finally saved by passage of the Endangered Species Act in 1973. The act outlawed all alligator hunting in the United States. Before long, alligator populations were out of danger. So strong was the animal's return, in fact, that Louisiana, Florida, and Texas reclassified the alligator on their endangered-species lists as having reached a stable population level and began allowing controlled hunts again in the mid-1970s. In late 1986, the USFWS proposed the reclassification of the alligator in seven other southern states.

Another more recent USFWS achievement concerns the red wolf, a species that once thrived in America's Southeast but reached near-extinction in the 1970s through interbreeding with coyotes and poisoning by area farmers. In 1978, under the Endangered Species Act, the USFWS removed the last surviving red wolves from the wild and placed them in a zoo, where they were successfully bred. Workers later moved the wolves to large pens in a North Carolina wildlife refuge and then released them there in 1987, where they produced cubs a year later. This animal was the first species previously extinct in the wild to reproduce after reintroduction to its natural habitat. This success ensured a future not only for the red wolf but also for many other endangered species that now exist only in captivity. In 1988 the Fish and Wildlife Service, working with the National Park Service, made similar plans to reintroduce another species, the gray wolf, to its former habitat in Yellowstone National Park.

The Battle for Control of American Lands

Preservationists seeking more stringent control of federally protected lands and the creation of new national parks and wilderness areas continue to fight an ongoing battle with those in favor of commercial and industrial development. In

The red wolf was the first endangered species to be bred in captivity and then successfully released into the wild. Its subsequent reproduction in its native habitat gave hope for the survival of other disappearing species.

James Watt:
A Controversial Secretary

When James Gaius Watt resigned from his post as secretary of the interior on October 9, 1983, his adversaries rejoiced. But despite this victory, they were wary of Watt's effect on Interior policy—and on the future of the nation's land and wildlife. In their view, during his two years in office Watt had abandoned concern for environmental protection and natural-resource preservation in favor of increased commercial use of government land. They further charged that his policies promoted unprecedented exploitation of the nation's resources and displayed a frightening disregard for wildlife, the environment, and the land itself.

Calls for Watt's removal began immediately upon his appointment to the post in 1981. Conservationists feared that Watt, the former head of the Mountain States Legal Foundation—a group accused by its critics of thwarting environmental regula-

tions in the interest of development—would begin yielding the nation's natural treasures to powerful industrial interests. Once Watt took office, his opponents saw this fear realized. He quickly moved to open many federally protected lands to commercial development.

Watt relaxed DOI regulation of strip mining, allowing him to accelerate the leasing of coal lands. Under his administration, millions of acres of public lands were opened to coal-mining companies. Conservationists charged that the haste with which these leases were granted increased the possibility of environmental damage. In addition, they claimed that the DOI was leasing the lands at an appallingly low price, at a loss to the government of possibly $100 million. Watt justified his actions by claiming that America needed to explore its mineral reserves in order to break its dependence on foreign re-

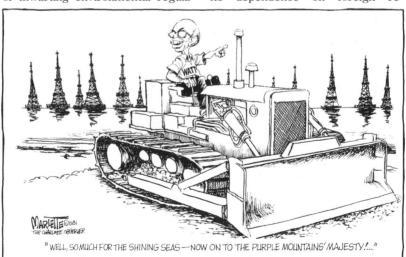

"WELL, SO MUCH FOR THE SHINING SEAS—NOW ON TO THE PURPLE MOUNTAINS' MAJESTY!...."

MARLETTE © 1982 THE CHARLOTTE OBSERVER

sources. He also argued that regulatory interference was keeping industry from this crucial resource development.

In his most controversial move, Watt took steps to open almost the entire U.S. coastline—1 billion acres on the outer continental shelf—to oil exploration. He asserted that risks to marine life and the coastline were minimal. His critics argued that numerous mishaps, such as the 1969 oil spill in Santa Barbara, California, suggested otherwise.

Watt channeled increased funds into the much-needed upkeep of facilities in the national parks. However, he declared a moratorium on the purchase of new parklands, even though Congress had already allocated funds for such land acquisition. Advocates for the national park system predicted that the delay in purchasing these areas meant that they would only be more expensive when purchased at a later date. Moreover, the DOI risked losing these lands

altogether because they might be sold to developers in the interim.

As the controversy over Watt's land-use policies grew steadily more bitter, he began to lose support even among his Republican allies. He further embarrassed himself and the Reagan administration with a series of miscalculated, often offensive attempts at humor. At best, Watt merely lacked diplomacy on such occasions; at worst, he displayed a cavalier insensitivity. Wildlife advocates winced at Watt's answer to the problem of coyote overpopulation: "Maybe we can get Mrs. Reagan to wear a coyote coat." But his most objectionable blunder was a 1983 comment about the diversity of a DOI coal-leasing review panel. Watt boasted that the panel included "a black, a woman, two Jews and a cripple." Soon after making this remark, Watt—a controversial political figure in an office controversial by nature—bowed to public pressure and resigned.

the early 1980s, the Interior Department came under attack from environmentalists and legislators who objected to the lenient land-use policies of President Ronald Reagan's secretary of the interior, James G. Watt. Appointed in 1981, Watt caused great controversy when he reduced DOI regulation in the area of environmental protection and allowed unprecedented exploitation of mineral and timber resources located on federal lands and on the outer continental shelf (submerged coastal lands). Watt was forced to resign in 1983, but his legacy has endured throughout the 1980s.

Debate rages over the use of public lands supervised by the DOI, primarily those areas located in the deserts and valleys of the West. The United States military conducts land and air training and weapons testing on such sites. Mining companies extract minerals from the land, and the public uses it for recreation. Ranchers rely on public lands to graze their sheep and cattle. These groups insist that their right to use these lands is crucial to the nation's economic well-being. Environmental groups charge, however, that such

Secretary of the Interior James Watt speaks before a governors' conference in 1983. The American public found Watt's federal land-use policies so objectionable that he was forced to resign later that year.

activities cause irreparable damage to the land and to the animals that live on it and that the DOI has failed in its duty to protect public lands from such abuses.

Friction continues between preservationists and advocates of development of America's national parks. Some environmental groups have called for the removal of all motels, hotels, concession stands, and other commercial enterprises now located within the parks. Hotels have been built in the national parks since the founding of the National Park Service in 1916; despite calls for their removal, the service claims that hotels and other businesses provide necessary services to those who visit the parks and pose little danger to the parks' scenic vistas and wildlife.

The Interior Department has also been charged with overzealous leasing of mineral rights to submerged coastal lands, a duty that is carried out by the DOI's Minerals Management Service. The growing number of leases granted to oil companies increases the likelihood of oil spills and air and water pollution in the areas surrounding offshore drilling operations. Some of these offshore drilling areas are also used as fishing grounds and for recreational use; marine life and nearby shoreline vegetation and wildlife are easily threatened by careless or excessive drilling.

Nevertheless, the Interior Department must continue to make crucial judgments concerning the balance between development—what certain interests insist is necessary progress—and preservation of the nation's lands and wildlife for the enjoyment of future generations. In its role as custodian of the nation's natural heritage, and as mediator between completely opposed forces, the DOI has historically found controversy; it will without doubt continue this tradition.

The bald eagle, America's national bird, is protected by endangered-species laws that are enforced by the USFWS. Nearly 500 varieties of U.S. animals and plants enjoy protection under this legislation.

FIVE

Responsibilities of the DOI

The Interior Department is 1 of 14 executive departments of the federal government directly responsible to the president. The secretary of the interior, the DOI's chief administrator, is a member of the president's cabinet. Appointed by the president and approved by the Senate, the secretary serves until he or she is replaced by the president or chooses to resign. Ultimately, the secretary is responsible for all action taken by the DOI.

The secretary of the interior is assisted by an under secretary, who acts as second in command and helps to discharge the secretary's duties. In the secretary's absence, the under secretary becomes acting secretary. Also under the supervision of the secretary of the interior are six assistant secretaries, each heading one of the six major divisions of the DOI: Fish and Wildlife and Parks; Indian Affairs; Land and Minerals Management; Territorial and International Affairs; Water and Science; and Policy, Budget, and Administration. Each assistant secretary has a staff of directors, associates, assistants, and other subordinates who conduct research, collect data, and decide how to use the nation's resources. Within the six divisions, duties are further divided into bureaus.

Polar bears on a wildlife refuge in Alaska. The U.S. Fish and Wildlife Service protects the nation's wildlife even in such remote areas as Alaska.

Fish and Wildlife and Parks

Perhaps the DOI's best-known function is to protect wildlife and parks. The assistant secretary for Fish and Wildlife and Parks has direct responsibility for programs involving development, conservation, and utilization of the nation's fish and wildlife resources and its recreational and historical national park systems. Under the assistant secretary's jurisdiction are two bureaus, each headed by a director and a deputy director. These are the U.S. Fish and Wildlife Service (USFWS) and the National Park Service (NPS).

The predecessor agencies to the U.S. Fish and Wildlife Service—the Bureau of Fisheries, established in 1871, and the Bureau of Biological Survey, created in 1885—were transferred to the DOI in 1939. Further reorganization led to the 1956 creation of the USFWS, a bureau charged with supervising efforts toward the conservation and protection of fish and wildlife and their habitats. The bureau now manages more than 400 national wildlife refuges, each of which provides a proper habitat for a host of different birds and animals. Among these are geese and ducks that migrate to different regions of the country as the seasons change. To protect some birds, USFWS hunting regulations determine the length of hunting seasons and limit the number of birds a hunter may kill. The regulations apply to various species, from the familiar doves, pigeons, and woodcocks to the lesser-known snipes and rails and cover birds using the four major routes—called *flyways*—that birds follow when migrating.

The USFWS carefully monitors wildlife population levels and acts to preserve a biological balance. If the population of a certain animal is observed to fall to a threateningly low level, the service will step in to keep the remaining population from becoming extinct—by classifying the animal as an endangered species in need of special protection. As of 1987, almost 500 U.S. mammal, reptile, crustacean, and plant species qualified as endangered. Once identified as such, these animals and plants receive USFWS protection, which promotes population growth to safe levels.

The U.S. Fish and Wildlife Service also administers federal grants for state fish-and-wildlife restoration programs. Through its fishery resource programs, the service operates national fish hatcheries that maintain population levels while allowing for recreational fishing. In addition, the service conducts programs to conserve and restore nationally significant fisheries and assists Indian tribes in the management of their fisheries.

A worker feeds fish at a U.S. Fish and Wildlife Service hatchery. The service operates hatcheries to restore fish population levels that have been depleted by illegal fishing, disease, excessive commercial development, and other abuses.

The National Park Service is perhaps the best-known division of the DOI. Since Congress established this agency in 1916, the nation's park system has grown into the largest of its kind in the world. Stretching across the country, the park system comprises more than 330 parks, monuments, historic sites, battlefields, seashores, and lakeshores. Park variety ranges from the rock-bound coast of Maine's Acadia National Park to the wind- and water-carved canyons, ridges, rock spires, and knobs of Badlands National Park in South Dakota—where bison, prairie dogs, and other native animals inhabit a remnant of the prairie that once stretched endlessly across North America's heartland—to the turquoise waters and sandy beaches of the Virgin Islands National Park.

The NPS ensures that these areas remain attractive and well maintained, protecting natural resources as well as cultural heritage for the enjoyment of the 250 million people who visit the parks each year. The NPS also provides a range of visitor services, including law enforcement, interpretation of park geology and history, and instruction about plant and animal life.

Many of the locations under the jurisdiction of the NPS figure significantly in the history of the nation. Some of these sites are ineligible for national park

Devil's Tower National Monument in Wyoming is an 865-foot-high rock tower with volcanic origins. The monument is under the jurisdiction of the National Park Service.

Monticello, Thomas Jefferson's home in Charlottesville, Virginia, is on the DOI's National Register of Historic Places. Although certain historically significant sites such as Monticello may be owned privately or by state governments, the DOI can ensure their legal protection from the construction of federally funded projects (such as airports or housing developments) by classifying them as national historic landmarks.

status because they are owned by other federal or state agencies, private organizations, or individuals. The secretary of the interior has the authority to designate such areas national historic landmarks. The Interior Department's register of national historic landmarks includes Mount Vernon, George Washington's home; and Monticello, Thomas Jefferson's home, both in Virginia, and various districts, sites, buildings, structures, and objects that hold significance in United States history, architecture, archaeology, and culture. By mid-1988, the number of national historic landmarks totaled 1,841.

Indian Affairs

Another of the DOI's critical concerns is Indian affairs. The assistant secretary for Indian affairs—a post created in 1977 by President Jimmy Carter and filled since its inception by Native Americans—is responsible for establishing department policy and monitoring ongoing programs concerning American

Indians and Indian affairs, identifying issues that affect Indian policy and programs, working with other federal agencies that provide funding or services to Indians, and overseeing the Bureau of Indian Affairs (BIA).

Created in 1824 as an agency of the War Department and transferred to the DOI when it was established in 1849, the BIA's principal responsibility is to promote self-management and advancement for Native American peoples, under a trust relationship with the federal government—an arrangement by which the government administers Indian lands and social services for the benefit of the tribes. Including Eskimo and Aleut natives of Alaska and the Aleutian Islands, about 1.4 million Native Americans live in the United States, according to the 1980 census. A 1985 Bureau of Indian Affairs study estimated that approximately 787,000 American Indians—more than half of the nation's total Indian population—live on or near a reservation.

The BIA's jurisdiction covers only members of officially recognized Indian tribes. Once the federal government officially acknowledges a tribe, the tribe

A group of Navajo children study a phonetic rendering of their native tongue at a BIA school in the 1940s. Education has historically been an important BIA service provided to reservation Indians.

Native Americans protest the relocation of Navajo Indians living in Arizona in 1986. Although the BIA works to promote the welfare of reservation Indians, the bureau has met with increasing criticism recently, and government treatment of American Indians is still highly controversial.

acquires certain rights and powers, including the right to federal aid and programs. A number of tribes have not gained federal recognition. Some groups do not want this recognition; others have been so isolated that few white people know they exist; still others have only a few members and are unable to press their demands. In 1987, there were 512 federally recognized Indian tribes in the United States; of these, about 300 have their own reservation. The largest, the Navajo Reservation, covers nearly 16 million acres in Arizona, New Mexico, and Utah. Some reservations, however, are as small as 100 acres.

To encourage the tribes to govern their own reservation communities, the BIA works with tribal governments to provide services that state and local governments usually provide. Among these are job training, road construction and maintenance, police protection, and welfare payment. The bureau also provides tribes with technical aid and services to help operate the reservations productively. Such BIA services include land management, forest development, leasing of mineral rights, direction of agricultural programs, and water- and land-rights protection. Providing education is another important BIA function: In 1987, the bureau operated 181 elementary and secondary schools with a total enrollment of 40,000 students and provided funding for 178,000 Indian students who attended public, private, and parochial (church-run) schools. In addition, the bureau funds 20 tribal community colleges and develops special programs in areas such as vocational training and adult education.

The BIA encourages tribes to take over and run their own programs once they are able to do so. In the early 1970s, for example, the BIA and Florida's Miccosukee tribe signed a contract giving the tribe power to run all educational and social services on its reservation. In 1983, President Ronald Reagan explained the motive for this working relationship in an American Indian policy statement: "Tribal governments are more aware of the needs and desires of their citizens than is the federal government," he said. They should therefore "have the primary responsibility for meeting those needs."

Land and Minerals Management

The DOI's assistant secretary for Land and Minerals Management is responsible for supervising the use of public lands and onshore and offshore mineral resources. The office also oversees surface mining and manages the collection of revenues from federal mineral leases. Three bureaus are under the supervision of this division: the Bureau of Land Management, the Office of Surface Mining Reclamation and Enforcement, and the Minerals Management Service.

The Bureau of Land Management (BLM) was established in 1946 by the consolidation of the General Land Office, created in 1812, and the Grazing Service, in operation since 1934. It is responsible for managing 270 million acres of public lands—about one-eighth of the total land area of the United States. (BLM lands are different from DOI holdings administered by the National Park Service or by the USFWS.) These lands are scattered throughout the country; however, the bulk of the BLM's jurisdiction falls in the West and in Alaska. Under the Federal Land Policy and Management Act of 1976, the BLM manages public-lands resources such as timber, hard minerals, oil and gas, and geothermal energy; wildlife habitats; endangered plant and animal species; rangeland vegetation; and recreation and wilderness areas. Bureau programs aim to protect, conserve, and develop public lands and their resources. The BLM is also responsible for supervision of land where mineral rights are owned by Indian tribes.

Whereas fish and wildlife agencies have responsibility for the wildlife itself, the BLM manages the wildlife habitats on public land. In protecting these wild animals, BLM functions often overlap with those of different DOI offices or separate government departments. For example, wild horses and burros are part of our American heritage. Legend claims that the first horses came to North America on Columbus's second voyage to the New World. Indians later used the animals to hunt buffalo, and explorers probed and settled the frontier on horseback. Cowboys, of course, depended on their horses to herd and drive cattle.

Burros were brought to the West by Jesuit missionaries and later used as pack animals by gold prospectors. Over the years, wild horse and burro herds grew as farmers and ranchers turned domesticated animals loose. Others ran away from wagon trains. After World War II, as wild herds flourished, commercial demand for horsemeat—for use in pet food—rose, and hunters

Wild horses, introduced into the New World in the 15th century, still roam public lands today. Such areas are under the supervision of the Bureau of Land Management and are used for a number of public and commercial activities, including recreation, mining, and ranching.

79

In strip mining, the top layer of soil is removed to expose the coal bed and is then replaced, after mining, for reclamation. Regulations developed by the Office of Surface Mining Reclamation and Enforcement ensure that this procedure is carried out responsibly and in keeping with environmental concerns.

began to chase the horses for profit. The resulting animal cruelty caused public outrage and prompted Congress to pass the Wild Free-Roaming Horse and Burro Act in 1971. Administered by the Interior Department's Bureau of Land Management and the Department of Agriculture's Forest Service, this law protects, manages, and controls wild horses and burros on public lands, recognizing their role in the country's past and assuring them a place in its future.

The Bureau of Land Management is also concerned with commercial land uses. The bureau leases publicly owned land to ranchers, mostly for raising cattle and sheep. Leasing revenues go to the U.S. Treasury as well as to state and local governments. Public forestlands also provide timber products that account for more than 1 billion board feet of lumber yearly.

Part of the nation's supply of coal, oil, and valuable minerals lies under public lands. The federal government leases some of this land to private companies.

Each year, these companies produce close to 115 million barrels of oil, almost a trillion cubic feet of natural gas, and more than 100 million tons of coal. They also mine smaller amounts of uranium, sodium, potash, and sulfur.

Coal mining, however, can damage land and water resources. In 1977, recognizing the environmental hazards of coal mining, Congress passed the Surface Mining Control and Reclamation Act, which established the Office of Surface Mining Reclamation and Enforcement (OSMRE), another bureau within the DOI's Office of Land and Minerals Management. The primary function of the OSMRE is to develop nationwide rules and standards to protect public health and the environment from the hazards of coal surface mining and to make sure that such mining is done without causing permanent damage to the nation's land and water resources. Based on minimum standards, each coal-mining state can set up regulations appropriate to its own special land conditions.

The third Land and Minerals Management bureau is the Minerals Management Service (MMS), created in 1982. The MMS supervises all outer continental shelf (OCS) mineral leasing, assessing mineral resources—their

Offshore oil drilling can be harmful to marine life and water quality. To protect the natural environment, the DOI's Minerals Management Service (MMS) oversees all mineral leasing on the outer continental shelf and conducts safety reviews of oil company operations.

American consultants on one of the Northern Mariana Islands aid native workmen in drilling a well. The Office of Territorial and International Affairs coordinates such federal aid programs in the U.S. territories.

nature, extent, recoverability, and value. It also develops 5-year oil- and gas-leasing programs in consultation with Congress, the 23 coastal states, local governments, environmental groups, industry, and the public. The MMS conducts environmental impact studies before granting a lease. After mining operations begin, MMS staff members conduct periodic inspections of offshore operations and collect data to ensure that the operation poses no hazard to the marine environment.

In addition to its supervisory duties, the MMS is also responsible for collecting and distributing all rentals, fines, and other monies due the federal government or Indian tribes from minerals leased on onshore federal or Indian lands and from the leasing and extraction of mineral resources on the OCS.

Territorial and International Affairs

Not all of the DOI's business pertains to the 50 United States. The Office of Territorial and International Affairs is responsible for promoting the economic, social, and political development of U.S. territories, including American Samoa, Guam, the Virgin Islands, the Commonwealth of the Northern Mariana Islands, and the Trust Territory of the Pacific Islands. The office coordinates federal policy in these areas and develops the federal budget for territorial activities. In addition, the office works with the assistant secretary of state for East Asian and Pacific Affairs to oversee all federal programs provided to the Freely Associated States (Marshall Islands and Federated States of Micronesia).

Water and Science

The Interior Department's fifth major division is Water and Science. The assistant secretary who heads this office is the science adviser to the secretary of the interior and is responsible for developing national water and mineral policies. The assistant secretary for Water and Science oversees the development and conservation of the nation's water supply; mineral data collection and analysis; departmental research in the earth sciences and in mining technology; and the programs of the Bureau of Mines, the U.S. Geological Survey, and the Bureau of Reclamation.

The Bureau of Mines, established in 1910, is primarily a research and statistics-gathering agency. The bureau collects statistical and economic information on resource development of minerals not used for fuel to confirm

Researchers at the Bureau of Mines use a scanning microscope to analyze field samples. The bureau is responsible for keeping track of the nation's nonfuel mineral resources.

that the nation has adequate supplies of these nonfuel minerals for security and other needs. (Of the approximately 80 minerals the bureau oversees—such as copper, iron, and chromium—34 are vital to the nation's economy and defense.) The bureau also examines data on exploration, production, shipments, demand, stocks, prices, imports, and exports of minerals, and publishes its findings. Many of the bureau's duties involve overseeing the research that provides technology for extracting, processing, using, and recycling nonfuel mineral resources in a cost-effective, environmentally safe manner.

The U.S. Geological Survey (USGS) is also a research-oriented organization. Established in 1879, the USGS spent its early years exploring the mountains and valleys of the West, mapping the wilderness and locating resources for utilization. Since then, it has evolved into the government's largest earth-science research agency. Today, the USGS is responsible for identifying the nation's land, water, mineral, and energy resources; classifying federal lands in terms of their resource potential; and investigating natural hazards such as earthquakes, volcanoes, and landslides. It is also the country's largest civilian mapmaking agency and the main data source for surface and groundwater resources information. More professional earth scientists work at the Geological Survey than anywhere else in the country.

The 1902 Reclamation Act created a program within the DOI to provide a year-round water supply to irrigate the arid western states. The Reclamation Service was originally placed within the U.S. Geological Survey; in 1907 the service was separated from the USGS, and in 1923 its name was changed to

Government mapmaking responsibilities fall to the U.S. Geological Survey, a department of the DOI with roots in the 19th-century wilderness surveys.

the Bureau of Reclamation. Today, the Bureau of Reclamation's dams, reservoirs, and canals provide water for towns, farms, and industries. For example, the Grand Coulee Dam on the Columbia River and the Hoover Dam on the Colorado River provide a year-round water supply for irrigation. Reservoirs also provide outdoor recreation such as fishing and swimming.

The Bureau of Reclamation oversees hydroelectric power generation (the production of electricity by waterpower), river regulation and flood control, and protection of fish and wildlife habitats. It inspects water quality and safety at its facilities, conducts environmental studies for proposed federal water-resource programs, and grants technical assistance to foreign countries in need of water-resource development.

Policy, Budget, and Administration

The assistant secretary for Policy, Budget, and Administration aids the secretary of the interior in management and administrative activities and serves as the secretary's principal policy adviser. As such, he or she provides detailed advice on programming, budget, and policy matters and develops administrative standards, objectives, and procedures for use throughout the department. In addition, the assistant secretary coordinates grants and organizational aspects of proposed legislation with the appropriate bureaus and offices. He or she is also responsible for such duties as emergency preparedness, law enforcement, financial management, printing of department publications, and personnel management.

Other Departmental Offices

In addition to the six assistant secretaries and the divisions they oversee, the DOI has other offices that are necessary to conduct business. These offices enable the department to conduct daily activities and long-range projects pertaining to the interior matters of the six divisions.

The Executive Secretariat is a secretarial tracking office, responsible for routing and monitoring all official correspondence to and from DOI staff members. The Executive Secretariat logs both incoming and outgoing mail and determines who among the staff should receive copies of the correspondence and who should prepare an answer. The Office of Congressional and Legislative

The Hoover Dam, completed in 1936, is located on the Colorado River between Nevada and Arizona. Under the supervision of the Bureau of Reclamation, the dam provides the region with flood control, river regulation, irrigation, and power.

Affairs is the DOI's congressional liaison. This office assists members of Congress in drafting legislation and keeps the DOI abreast of relevant congressional activities. The Public Affairs Office communicates information on DOI programs and initiatives to the media and to the public and coordinates the efforts of the public-affairs officers in all DOI bureaus and at field stations.

The Office of the Solicitor, or legal adviser, is responsible for the department's legal work. The solicitor supervises six divisions, each headed by an associate solicitor and qualified to work with the concerns of specific DOI subdivisions. For example, the office's Division of Conservation and Wildlife handles legal matters for the assistant secretary for Fish and Wildlife and Parks, the National Park Service, and the U.S. Fish and Wildlife Service. Other divisions may include bureaus from separate DOI offices.

The Office of Inspector General is responsible for maintaining the integrity of DOI operations. Reporting directly to the secretary of the interior, the inspector general coordinates internal audit and investigation services, identifying and prosecuting possible cases of fraud or abuse within the department. The inspector general also supervises relations between the DOI and other federal, state, and local government agencies concerning promotion of economy and efficiency, prevention and detection of fraud and abuse, and prosecution of people charged with these crimes.

The Office of Hearings and Appeals carries out departmental appeals procedures. The director of this office supervises administrative law judges and three formal boards of appeal that render decisions in cases pertaining to a variety of matters, including contract disputes and conflicts over Indian wills and estates, public lands and resources, offshore oil leases, surface coal-mining control and reclamation, and importation and transportation of rare and endangered species.

The Office for Equal Opportunity (OEO) is responsible for the development and enforcement of civil rights and equal opportunity programs concerning contracting and employment rights, under federal statutes that prohibit discrimination on the basis of race, color, age, sex, national origin, handicap, or religion. Headed by a director who reports to the under secretary, the OEO advises the secretary of the interior and the bureaus and offices within the DOI on all matters of equal opportunity and civil rights.

The Office of Small and Disadvantaged Business Utilization coordinates all DOI matters relating to small, disadvantaged, and minority businesses. This office conducts outreach seminars for small and disadvantaged businesses and works with other government agencies such as the Small Business Administration, the Office of Federal Procurement Policy, the Minority Business Development Agency, and the General Services Administration. The department's director reports to the under secretary and assists DOI bureaus and offices in developing policies and carrying out procedures relating to these businesses.

The Office of Youth Programs oversees DOI programs of employment and training for young people. Programs administered by this office include the Job Corps Civilian Conservation Centers Program and the U.S. Youth Conservation Corps. The director is responsible for coordinating programs with related federal departments—such as Agriculture and Labor—and for making sure that the programs are responsive to Congress and to the public.

The variety of functions performed by the DOI requires a complex structure of divisions and bureaus. Yet all are linked by the common goal of protecting and managing the nation's resources, both cultural and natural, for the benefit of all.

Park rangers at Gettysburg National Military Park, the site of an 1863 Civil War battle. The National Park Service staff provides valuable services to visitors, including interpreting park vegetation and wildlife and leading tours.

SIX

The Future of the DOI

There are many examples of the ways in which the DOI has achieved its mandate for the benefit of the public and the nation. National parks provide recreation and enjoyment; historic sites commemorate important events in American history; and endangered species lists protect wildlife and the natural environment. Judging the overall success of the department, however, is not as simple.

The plight of American Indians still troubles the nation's conscience. Although the present department is performing much-needed functions for Indians, it has not always been as helpful. The bloody confrontations of the 19th century on the Great Plains and other abuses in the 20th century have fostered bitterness and misunderstanding, which the department must work to alleviate. And despite the progress made in some areas of federal Indian policy, many reservation communities continue to be plagued by problems. In recent years critics have charged that the BIA has persistently failed to deal adequately with health problems, economic mismanagement, and other difficulties on the reservations.

In the 1980s, the habitat of these caribou and other arctic wildlife species was threatened by imminent oil exploration in Alaska's Arctic National Wildlife Refuge. The conflict over proposals to develop the area is characteristic of the tension between developers and preservationists with which the Interior Department must contend.

While the DOI continues to address the problems it has faced in the past, it will also meet new challenges. For example, throughout the 1980s there was an ongoing conflict between environmental-protection advocates and resource developers in Alaska. According to many geologists, the nation's last large oil deposit lies under the coastal plain of Alaska's 18-million-acre Arctic National Wildlife Refuge. Oil experts claim that the area has the potential to be an immense storehouse of crude oil reserves. Interior Department officials agree. In fact, the nation's largest oil field, Prudhoe Bay Field, is only 60 miles away from the refuge.

However, the wildlife refuge also contains breathtaking scenery and is home to many animal species, including the nation's largest caribou herd. The question facing the Interior Department is whether it should open the refuge's coastal plain for the development of oil and gas and thereby risk endangering its land and animal life. Environmental-protection groups have compared this prospect to damming the Grand Canyon to get hydroelectric energy or to tapping Yellowstone's geothermal energy. Resolving this dilemma without discounting the concerns of either the environmentalists or those who claim that the nation desperately needs the area's fuel resources will require a great deal of thought and action on the part of the DOI.

Another environmental problem facing the country in the 1980s is that of nuclear-waste disposal. Radioactive waste from nuclear reactors, which produce electricity for use in American homes and industry, has been building up for decades; this waste can be harmful to humans, animals, and the environment if it is not safely disposed of. Skeptics question the basic safety of any kind of nuclear-waste disposal. After nuclear accidents in 1979 at Pennsylvania's Three Mile Island plant and in 1986 at the Chernobyl nuclear power plant in the Soviet Union, critics have challenged the safety of nuclear power plants themselves. Deciding how to deal with the hazards posed to the nation's land and wildlife by nuclear reactors and their waste products will continue to demand the DOI's attention.

A different kind of issue the department will address is the political nature of the secretary. As the president's appointee, the secretary answers to the president rather than to the public; in the 1980s, this situation has caused increasing political problems. In 1983, environmentalists repeatedly clashed with Interior Secretary James Watt over his exploitive land-use policies. Opposition did not cease until Watt resigned. Later, in 1988, a bill was introduced in Congress that would remove the National Park Service from the jurisdiction of the secretary of the interior and make it an independent agency.

One of the many dangers to public and environmental health today is the unsafe disposal of radioactive waste generated by nuclear power plants. Protecting the nation from such threats will continue to be a challenge to the Interior Department.

Because the director of the NPS is appointed by the interior secretary—who is a political appointee—and reports directly to him or her, critics both within the NPS and outside its staff feel that the service cannot objectively carry out its mandate unless it is independent of political interference. Whether such a change is truly needed, and whether it would indeed succeed in removing the nation's parks system from the political arena, remains to be seen.

Environmentalists and the general public demand accountability for DOI actions. Response to public needs is the foundation of the department's history and its basis for past successes. Under pressure to meet the public's various—and often conflicting—needs, the department will continue in its efforts to preserve the nation's natural heritage.

Department of the Interior

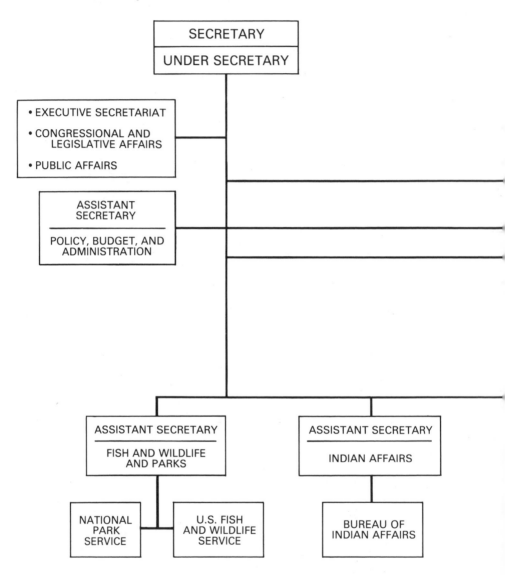

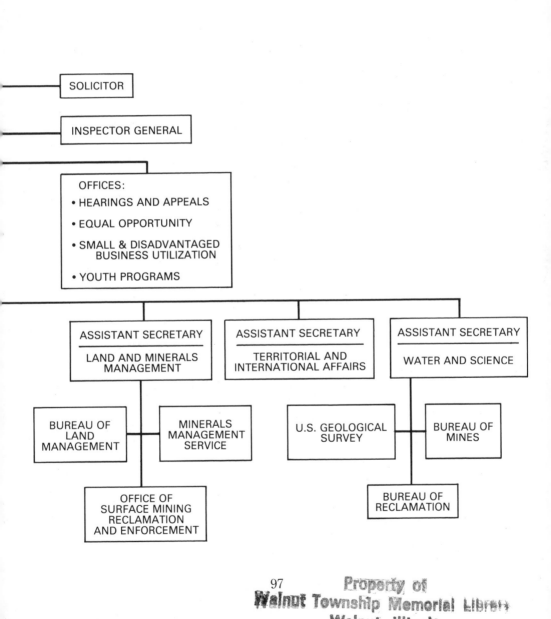

Property of
Walnut Township Memorial Library
Walnut, Illinois

GLOSSARY

Conservation   The careful preservation of natural resources to prevent their deterioration or destruction.

Endangered species   An animal species whose population has been reduced to the point where it is in danger of becoming extinct.

Environmental protection   The action of keeping the existing environment safe from poisons and pollutants by focusing on the dangerous effects of man-made materials.

Extinct   No longer existing; animal species in danger of extinction are protected by U.S. Fish and Wildlife Service endangered species laws.

Flyway   An established air route of migratory birds.

National historic landmark   A site, building, or object of significant historic interest that is officially designated and set aside for preservation.

National park   An area of special scenic, historic, or scientific importance set aside for preservation and maintained by the federal government.

Pesticide   A chemical agent used to destroy agricultural pests; because of various harvesting techniques pesticides may contaminate some foods.

Reservation   An area of land reserved by the federal government for use by recognized Indian tribes.

Survey   To examine and record the physical characteristics of an area by taking measurements and by applying the principles of geometry and trigonometry.

Wildlife refuge   An area set aside by the federal government to preserve that area or protect a species of wildlife in its natural habitat.

SELECTED REFERENCES

Alexander, Thomas G. *A Clash of Interests: Interior Department and Mountain West, 1863–1896*. Provo, UT: Brigham Young University Press, 1977.

Carson, Rachel. *Silent Spring*. Boston: Houghton Mifflin, 1962.

Dolin, Eric Jay. *The U.S. Fish and Wildlife Service*. New York: Chelsea House, 1989.

Forness, Norman O. "The Origins and Early History of the U.S. Department of the Interior." Ph.D. dissertation. Philadelphia: Pennsylvania State University, 1964.

Gates, Paul W., and Robert W. Swenson. *History of Public Land Law Development*. Washington, D.C.: Ayer Co., 1979.

Graham, Frank, Jr. *Man's Dominion: The Story of Conservation in America*. New York: M. Evans & Company, 1971.

Mackintosh, Barry. *The National Park Service*. New York: Chelsea House, 1988.

Porter, Frank W., III. *The Bureau of Indian Affairs*. New York: Chelsea House, 1988.

Smith, Frank E. *The Politics of Conservation: The First Political History of the Conservation and Development of America's Natural Resources*. New York: Pantheon Books, 1966.

Trani, Eugene P. *Secretaries of the Interior, 1849–1969*. Washington, D.C.: National Anthropological Archives, 1975.

U.S. Department of the Interior. *America 200: The Legacy of Our Lands*. Washington, D.C.: U.S. Government Printing Office, 1976.

Utley, Robert M., and Barry Mackintosh. *The Department of Everything Else: Highlights of Interior History*. Washington, D.C.: The U.S. Department of the Interior, 1988.

INDEX

Polk, James K., 27, 33
Pollution, 58–59
Post Office, Department of the, 20
Powell, John Wesley, 40, 41

Radioactive waste disposal, 93
Reagan, Ronald, 78
Reclamation Service, 46, 85
Red wolves, 64–65
Rocky Mountains, 40
Roosevelt, Franklin D., 51
Roosevelt, Theodore, 46–47

Sanford, Nathan, 21
Schurz, Carl, 42
Silent Spring (Carson), 58–59
Sitting Bull, 45
Smith, Joseph, 26–27
South Dakota, 36
State, Department of, 20, 21
Surface Mining Control and Reclamation Act of 1977, 81
Sutter, Johann Augustus, 35

Texas, 26, 28
Timber Culture Act of 1873, 42
Treasury, Department of the, 20, 24, 31

Udall, Stewart L., 57–58
Utah, 27

Virgin Islands National Park, 74

Walker, Robert J., 31–32, 33
War, Department of, 20, 41, 76
Water Pollution Control Act of 1956, 58
Watt, James G., 68, 93
West, Roy O., 16
Wheeler, George M., 41
Wild Freeroaming Horse and Burro Act of 1971, 80
Wilderness
  cattle grazing in, 68–69
  commercial use of, 55–56, 65–69
  Douglas McKay's policy concerning, 53–54
  military use of, 68
  mining in, 68, 69
  protection of, 55–58
  surveying of, 37–41
Wilderness Act of 1964, 57
Wildlife protection, 62–65, 72–73, 93

Yellowstone National Park, 41–42, 65, 93

Fred Clement, a free-lance writer, holds a degree in English from Princeton University. He has previously worked as a reporter and editor and has won several Pennsylvania journalism awards, including a 1979 Keystone Press Award for the best news story and, in 1984, the Jesse H. Neal Editorial Achievement Award. He is the author of *The Nuclear Regulatory Commission*, another volume in the KNOW YOUR GOVERNMENT series published by Chelsea House.

Arthur M. Schlesinger, jr., served in the White House as special assistant to Presidents Kennedy and Johnson. He is the author of numerous acclaimed works in American history and has twice been awarded the Pulitzer Prize. He taught history at Harvard College for many years and is currently Albert Schweitzer Professor of the Humanities at the City College of New York.

Property of
Walnut Township Memorial Library
Walnut, Illinois

PICTURE CREDITS:

American Petroleum Institute: cover, p. 81; AP/Wide World Photos: pp. 49, 52, 57, 61, 68, 80; Bettmann Archive: p. 43; Clarence King: p. 39; Library of Congress: pp. 16, 18, 20, 22, 23, 24, 25, 26, 28, 29, 30, 32, 34, 36, 38, 40, 41, 44, 45, 46, 50, 51, 87; National Park Service: cover, pp. 2, 14, 48, 55, 56, 64, 90; National Park Service/Richard Frear: p. 94; National Park Service/William Keller: pp. 70, 74; New Bedford Standard Times/Staff Photo: p. 60; Office of Territorial and International Affairs: p. 82; Donna Sinisgalli: p. 27; United States Bureau of Land Management: p. 79; United States Bureau of Mines: p. 84; United States Geological Service: p. 85; UPI/Bettmann News-photos: pp. 54, 59, 62, 63, 76, 77; United States Fish and Wildlife Service (USFWS): p. 65; USFWS/Gerry Atwell: p. 72; USFWS/Keith Morehouse: p. 92; USFWS/Robert Shallenberger: p. 17; USFWS/Tom Smylie: p. 73; Virginia Division of Tourism: p. 75